1 IWACU

How can I begin to tell you the story about Iwacu, where I was born? How can one write about life and the genocide that we have survived in the same page? How can you convey the terrible moments of being a witness to the devils in darkness? As I was writing this book, my friend asked me to create sounds that echoed the loss of life and pain I experienced during the Tutsi genocide in Rwanda. It is still a question: "How"? How can you recreate the memory of genocide No matter what you answer, it is true because the past shapes our perceptions of today and tomorrow.

You might discover many answers to your questions as you read my memoir. Or, it may leave you with many more. There are many questions about humanity because of what my family, my neighbors, and I witnessed that was beyond the comprehension of the human mind. From the 1959 deportation to Nyamata, I'm talking about years of humiliation and dehumanization, as well as torture, killing, and alienation.

My parents survived the 1959 and 1960s massacres. They rebuilt their lives and instilled hope in our children. My father, my younger brother and nearly my entire family were killed in the 1994 genocide. I was devastated by what had happened to my childhood. Writing and sharing my story with others was the only way to preserve these memories forever. Most survivors have a voice in their heads that tells them that they were not allowed to tell the truth, as Immacule Iribagiza1 wrote about her experience with the genocide.

This story tells me how I escaped from machetes, wood clubs, grenades and other weapons used by the Interahamwe Hutu militia, gendarmes and communal police to kill my people. However, it is not my testimony. It's about the memories of the Rwandans who were killed in 1994 and the strength of the survivors. It is a journey that I

Share with you a piece of my life, which I lost when my entire family died in the dark, smokey church of Nyamata. The Bugesera region was once occupied by concentration camps for Tutsis from northern Rwanda. This is the area where my father was born. I hope that this book will reflect the years in which my father and his family were expelled to the Savannah.

This is a story about my childhood, Nyirarukobwa, Rwangara and the stories they told. It's about the dark times that I lived in the beautiful hills of Kayumba or Karambi where nightmares were a reality. It also describes the rainy and sunny days spent in the forest, and the nights and days spent in the bushes. It's about the massacre of Tutsi women, men, and children inside the Catholic Church in Nyamata. This place became symbolic of hundreds of other churches that were transformed into refuges for Tutsis, but then turned into graveyards.

Genocide isn't about numbers, it is about lives, culture, and memories of exterminated persons. This account is about our lives in Bugesera, and the lives that we lost in Nyamata in those dark days when God was believed to spend his daylight hours outside, and sleep peacefully in the land of one million hills. But he never returned. It's about the Nyamata Genocide Memorial that holds my memories. I fled the site on 16 April 1994, having survived the massacre that claimed 10,000 lives in the Nyamata Catholic Church, its compound, Sunday Schools, and convents. It's about Antonia Locatelli (an Italian nun who alerted the international community in 1992 to the fact that Tutsis had been systematically murdered in Bugesera). Similar events were taking place in Bigogwe, Kibirira and other regions. The Nyamata Memorial includes her cemetery. It reminds people that the victims of Nyamata's brutal massacres and systematic murders that took place since

1963. Because she attempted to rescue those who fled to Nyamata Church, she was shot to death. We had already stopped attending Nyirarukobwa Primary School at the time. My family did not reach Nyamata because Locatelli's murder became well-known, and the Government of Habyarimana was forced to stop the massacre.

How can these terrible events have occurred? Although the answer is a puzzle to human logic, I suspect that you may have similar thoughts as you read this story about me and my survival. Sometimes, it can be difficult to create such images in the mind of a reader. Bugesera, an area in the southeast part of Rwanda, is located between Akagera and Nyabarongo rivers and near the border to Burundi.

Burundi is full of stories. This area was once home to Bugesera's people, but it also housed lions and elephants as well as other animals. After fleeing their burned homes in Ndusu, Bukonya, they moved to Ruhengeri, northern Rwanda, to find safety. They were then deported to Nyamata by the Belgian colonial administration in December 1959.

Officially, Rwanda was still under Belgian colonial administration at that time. They spent two years in Nyamata refugee camps (1959-1961) which were difficult. But, it is not easy to be a refugee. My mother Nyinawumwami married my father in Bugesera after having suffered a similar trauma in the 1960s. After losing their entire property and previous happiness, my parents left behind the shocking memories I inherited as a child.

These memories manifested in the form of pain in their eyes and stories. As I grew up, their grief and psychological wounds were present in my life. This was evident from my mother's silence regarding the past to my dad's conversations with neighbours to the surrounding environment. They did everything possible to provide for me and my younger brother and sister, despite all their hardships. They are my heroes, they are always in my heart.

As a child, I was fascinated by my family's story of Nyamata's initial days and their eventual settlement in Bugesera.

Flashbacks were a part of my autobiographical story. I realized that I would need to have real conflicts in order to be able capture the essence of this story. This is why I felt a book about my time in Nyamata was unfair if it only covered my experience during the genocide.

I wanted to tell the stories of my family's hardships in the 1960s and, most importantly, my dad's deportation from Nyamata refugee camps. This was a life that I had never lived, and I wasn't physically there. So I was left wondering: How do I include stories from a time that I didn't belong to? These stories were my own. Their ghosts kept reminding of me that they were a part my dark life. A life I never lived and never got a chance explore.

Writing helped me to see how my parents' story during their first days in Bugesera shaped my whole life. These accounts were the real problem. The issue remained unresolved to the end of the chronicle.

In my endless conversation with myself about my past I realized how Nyamata had taken away my wonderful childhood memories. My childhood memories of my time with my family, the happy times at Nyirukobwa Primary school, playing with other children around our neighborhood, and trips to Kurarete (Arete), centre with Burandine and Nyiranuma had disappeared into my subconscious. Kurarete, our lovely little town's centre, is still a busy small business hub that attracts people from Kigali, Kukibungo and Ntarama as well as from the nearby villages of Kizunguruko and Kukibungo. People used to wake up early to buy and sell crops, as well as traditional beer (urwagwa) in Kinyarwanda. I can still remember the old Toyotas returning to Kigali loaded with urwagwa, crops, and other goods. How could I have forgotten these days and only remember the dark times of Nyamata. I was reminded by writing this autobiographical account that just because you survived a genocide doesn't mean you have to forget them. They remain in your subconscious forever. Everything you see, hear, or remember reminds of both your beautiful and dark past. How can you live your present, future and past with a sense that shock lingers?

My writing was more difficult the deeper my thoughts were. My childhood was the first thing I saw. Habamungu Ramadhan my father shared with me how his family was forced to leave their land and how his brother Munyensanga, who was later killed in Nyabarongo, was taken away. He also explained how Uwamaliya Renatha, his daughter of two months, was left behind. All the unanswered questions that I kept asking myself made me curious. I was curious about how they left their homes to move to Bugesera, a land filled with savannah forests, animals, and what their homes looked like. These were questions I was raised asking, but never getting answers.

It's not easy to remember, but the dream of sharing our lives and the lives lost at Nyamata was what drove me to wake up every morning to write the unimaginable. How can I tell you my story and let go of my trauma?

I eventually came to terms that I was a survivor, born to survivors. My father survived cholera and malaria, pneumonia, and other diseases that killed many in Nyamata's camp. He also survived the killings of 1960s when my maternal grandfather was imprisoned for being Inyenzi (Cockroaches).

It was hard to remember a past that you have not lived, and any representation of it is a constructed image from your own sources and insufficient. However, I realized that the reason I kept trying to tell the story through my eyes was because it becomes a story about hope. I have the hope that your yesterday will not be forgotten by you reading it here.

This work will serve as an example of how to create images from the past that can be used for the faces of the future.

This story is not about me and my family, but it does add to the literature on the persecution of Tutsis during the period of 1963, 1964 and 1968.

Many people lost their lives in these massacres. Then came a life of hardship in refugee camps both inside and outside of the country. Uwamaliya Renatha is my cousin. She lost her father in 1963 and was left an orphan. It was the most difficult part of trying to relate to something I had read in a portion of a speech from former President Gregoire Kayibanda on 29 April 1963:

"You've seen the recent disturbances caused by the Inyenzi refugees' indiscipline, and wickedness. This is something that the Nyamata population and Bufundu population know. This can be attributed to the secular wickedness that feudalism has instilled. "The November 1959 abyss continues to grow for the feudal and his aides." 2 This speech summarized everything I remember.

This journey, which I shared filled with sad stories and self-discovery led me to discover the reasons behind my hesitation to return to this terrible past. I chose to share it with other scholars and authors. It was terrifying to go into my subconscious and confront those rainy, bloody nights and days when human beings were turned in to corpses by Interahamwe Hutu militia who behaved like wolves and competed about who had killed the most children and women!

One would assume that survivors have stories to tell. Many survivors' stories are filled with the phrase "I thought those days were my last days." It's almost like reliving the story of a horror movie, complete with serial killers and many dark scenes. Shared experiences are the best comfort for survivors. It is almost like reliving the plot of a horror movie with serial killers, with endless dark episodes?

My friend Stephanie Wolfe invited me to speak to her students at Weber State University in Ogden (Utah) in 2019. It was a pleasure to have a platform to share some of my experiences. My first day at the University Garden, I noticed that she had given my talk the title "Life and death in Nyamata". She also included my photograph on the billboard. It was so moving to see this. It was on our return trip home that we first saw the billboard. I was stunned.

 She said, "Oh, that's you.".

We stopped to take a few photos. It was both scary and exciting for me, as this was my first English talk in front of an audience. But I was glad to share the darkness and joy of Nyamata with these American students. After returning from Utah, I decided that I would write about this terrible part of my life and name it Life and Death in Nyamata.

It seemed to be enough to sum up the life I lived with memories of silent souls. This book tells the story of how I survived a crime Raphael Lemkin could not name, and why he invented the term "genocide". How do you depict the horror, pain, humiliation and cruelty that comes with genocide? How can you normalize the dehumanization that genocide brought about? Sometimes, it's difficult to convey through words the reality we saw from those without human faces.

This narrative is the culmination of past memories and my nightmares. It pushed me to share my story of survival of the genocide with others, who might visit Nyamata Genocide Memorial someday. Because reading a book about a survivor's story is like listening to them, and there is nothing more therapeutic than dedicating your time to sharing these stories with others, I owe you all a lot.

My memoir was also inspired by meeting other authors who were interested in Nyamata's story, and with whom I shared my story for their books.

It was also a request from close and dear friends, who supported me in writing about my Nyamata life. As I tell you about the origins of this book, I should mention Kate Etzel, her daughter Sarah Etzel, and their efforts to ensure that this book was published. This book was made possible by their hard work.

Sarah was a student I was supervising at Never Again Rwanda. This NGO is a local peacebuilding and prevention NGO. Our work together was in the Youth Engagement and Empowerment unit. After we had discussed my drafts, she shared them with Kate, her beautiful mother, who was determined to help me find a publisher. She would add, "I will make your dream come true." We were both thrilled to receive a reply from Liesbeth, who stated that Amsterdam Publishers would be interested!

Kate and Sarah Etzel, my dear friends Samantha Lakin, Dr. Sara E.Brown and Prof. Stephanie Wolfe are the true reason this book exists.

Again, I believe reading this long and emotional account makes you stronger. It shows us a side to human beings that we didn't know existed. Thank you so much for taking the time to read about my experiences in Nyamata, Rwanda and other areas during the genocide. It is something that I will never forget. This book is a testament to my grief; it also forecasts the future. After surviving the genocide, I felt that being optimistic about the future was the best choice.

I ask that you stand by me and offer a prayer to those who have lost their lives in this tragedy of humanity. This autobiographical account is about sharing and keeping alive the memories of my people. We will be traveling together from Iwacu up to Nyamata, where smiling children and cattle were once replaced with the blood that flowed through the swamps of Bugesera or other parts of Rwanda.

This autobiography was written to share my experiences with you, but also to preserve the memories of those who have lost their lives due to what they didn't choose to be. My oral Rwandan culture required that I share my stories with all people I spoke to. But it wasn't enough. My inner voice kept calling for more, until Professor Stephanie Wolfe suggested that we write a book about Nyamata. These voices were always present in my head. I wanted to write a book about Nyamata, preserving their stories, their clothes and everyday items, as well their memories, so future generations could see what happened. Stephanie initially suggested that we write on eight national memorials. However, we decided to expand our work to include 265 Rwandan genocide memorials. We wanted to tell stories about the final days of those in memorials through the eyes of those who managed to escape before their voices were silenced in churches and government offices, on the streets, and in the hills. You will probably understand why Stephanie and I decided to publish Journey through Rwandan Memorials together after we met in 2014. Because it was such an enormous task dealing with collective memories, we agreed to include Dr. AnnaMarie de Beer as well as Dr. Joseph Nkurunziza. We climbed up the hills of Rwanda to listen to survivors' stories, stopping at times to cry about their losses. I was able to see the relevance of this book as we went. It was difficult for me to do this as a survivor. Every letter from their testimony reminded me of 1994's dark days, when night was all that was possible and it was impossible to move about.

Nyamata was easy to carry once I had written these words. I had spent my time listening to the past and Nyamata was an easy burden to carry. Writing this book has helped me to listen to myself. Since the genocide, I have kept my soul hidden away with the memories of the church of Nyamata, the sounds of bullets, wooden club and machetes crushing heads and necks of Tutsi people, as if it was their choice. Writing was how I healed. My computer had become my safe place, a refuge, which allowed me to share my story with you!

Writing this account made it clear to me that writing about your personal life is a school that offers many options for you, even regarding your past. It is a refuge from many questions I had about my past. I also use it to visualize and immortalize my memories. I believe collective memories can become a monument to the past. Felicitee Lyamakuru is a Nyundo genocide survivor. I wrote this in my copy of L'ouragan a frappe Nyundo (A Storm Has Hit Nyundo), which she launched in 2018. La memoire est ce qui faire l'Homme et l'histoire de Notre est a preserver. enrichir et meme souver... Stay brave.

These words were precious words to close this introduction. Impore is an acronym for bravery and courage. This account is mine. It means you are listening to me. It is important to me because, in the words Prof. Naasson's words, "the misfortune of not having no one listens to you while there is a world filled with people". You are a great source of gratitude for your understanding and compassion.

2 MY CHILDHOOD

Every child treasures childhood memories, so I consider my early years to be a wonderful time. I was raised in a family that included relatives my age and older. Blandine, Nyiranuma and Uncle Callixte were my age, so I loved playing with them. Callixte also had older children, including Ntirenganya and Paul,

Mufabure, who were assistant Bourgmestres of the former community of Kanzenze), Kigingi and Uwizeye. Theophile was the firstborn, who lived in Kigali, the capital. I had a great time playing kwihishanwa (hiding game), and other games with Uwihirwe and Umutoni, who were also my relatives. Evase Kabanda was a son we all loved and admired. He would build small houses out of mud and branches that could hold one child.

My unforgettable time with Uncle Karemera Dominiko is something I will never forget. He was a priest at Kanzenze Catholic Church, a teacher at Nyirukobwa Primary school, and a senior catechist at Nyirarukobwa High School. This school, which was the only one in the area, served thousands of students from Nyirarukobwa, and the hills surrounding, since the 1960s. I used to play agati1and kwihishanwa with Gloriose, Claude Shimwa and Lambert, and also sing songs with Petero. My uncle Karemera was the father of all these children. Fils, Monica and Rukara were his older children. They were too old to play with him.

In those dark nights, we were able to socialize, talk with parents, and recite guca imigani (fables), and other children's stories, thanks to the light of the moon. Electricity had not yet reached our village. We all enjoyed sitting together as children in the same house to talk. Karemera was a favorite of ours, especially during gukama (milking). We were often found near Musengo or Kijyambere. These are the sweetest and most adorable cows Uncle Karemera Dominiko, and his wife Yozefa. We children could drink the last kigozi of milk. I would then walk home in the darkness.

Our family didn't have everything, but we had enough to live. I was thankful for the love of my parents, even though their lives were reassembled from scratch. My father was a farmer and a salesman. My time with my father was precious to me as a child. Nyinawumwami was my mother. She had a difficult childhood and loved to encourage us to work hard. Ntugakore ku ijisho (Never let others see you work, but work hard), was her favorite saying. I was her firstborn and I quickly began to help her with various domestic chores. Sometimes I wished that I could finish faster to be able to play karere (a game with a ball made of banana leaves). This was our time to relax and enjoy our childhood and games.

Many children from our village became friends because their parents had been through similar events. I was a classmate at primary school and knew Habarugira and Uwamaliya's children Olivier, Mignone and Fillete. We would play together when they visited. Narcisse's children, Kadinde and Robin, Minette, Tata, Tata, and the very young Budodo were all there. My mother, Aline Narcice, was close to me. It was a lovely neighborhood with good memories.

I still remember the nights we would run in darkness trying to catch insects with our glasses. I loved the ones that lit up in the dark at night. I spent hours trying to catch them. Bugesera was a part of Bugesera. Some people still hunt wild animals, particularly wild rabbits. The time was amazing when your peers wouldn't play with you if you were wearing shoes because they thought it would cause injury to their legs. Although being late home would result in punishment, we were usually on time.

I was invited to play with Maliya Muzyirwa's grandchildren, Pusi, and Binyagu. We had lots of fun and our karere balls were very large. It was dark when I returned home and my mother was angry. As she was about beating me, I ran to Callixte. My mum arrived at the house a few hours later and, screaming, said that she was taking me home. My heart was beating fast because I knew coming home would mean punishment. When I arrived home, I called my father. But I knew my mother wouldn't tolerate my insolence. I fell asleep after I was punished. All children learn from their mistakes.

My family was Catholic, but I grew up in an Islamic family. After he moved to Bugesera in 1970s, my father converted to Islam. He used to take me to Ntarama as a child. Gasasira Seman, a wealthy and well-known Muslim man, gave up his home to make it a mosque where Muslims could pray and learn the Quran. It was difficult to get there as we lived so far away.

My favorite thing about going with my dad to Jummah prayers Fridays, was stopping by the restaurant for tea. My cousins and other peers attended Kanzenze Catholic Church. I was unable to tell the difference between Islam and Christianity as a child.

Later, I realized that this was an opportunity to grow up in two religions. This made me more open to other faiths. My family's religious situation was also a result of 1959's deportation of the Tutsi from Bugesera. My father decided years ago to leave Bugesera and go to Nyamilambo where he converted to Islam from Catholicism. As a child, I was surrounded by my family and friends, so the differences between religions weren't too noticeable except during Ramadan. I once went to Maliya's home and was served meat and ubugali by her granddaughters. My father saw my hands when I returned from Maliya's house and asked me to wash them. Then he smelled my skin.

"What have your eaten?" He asked.

"Meat, we ate in Maliya Muuzayirwa's house."

That was a terrible time. My father must have smelled pork meat, which I didn't know.

He said, "I'll beat your so that you won't eat pork again.".

I said, "I will not do it again.".

To make sure that I don't do it again, he punished me. This was how I found out that pork was forbidden in my faith. It was something I would never do again.

Those days with my father taught me a lot. I used to sit beside him and listen to the news in Swahili and Kinyarwanda, pretending sometimes that a box was my radio. He was calm and enjoyed listening to radio and talking with his friends. Nyamata or Ntarama Muslims would sometimes visit our neighborhood to preach and pray. Ramadan was the religious festival I loved most during my childhood. I would fast for half a year and then exhaust my parents because I wanted to eat at idaku. As a child, the best thing was waking up with my parents. They taught me so much and I never thought I'd be where I am today without them. Although they were strict disciplinarians and hard workers, I loved our time together. This is where I got my work ethic.

* * *

My childhood memories are filled with laughter and fun. This involved a table that was drawn on the ground using small squares and two semicircles at each end. These memories take me back.

Each morning and evening, we were to fetch water from Nyamihana's pump. It was located in Nyirukobwa swamp. Not being the first to arrive did not necessarily mean that you got your water first. Older boys might practice inkomoti. Inkomoti is a game where you push each other. Sometimes it led to fighting until one of the stronger participants had pulled away all others to fetch water. This game had no rules, only pure strength was what mattered. We were told to get up early in order to arrive at the water pump earlier than others. Sometimes, I would ask inkomoti practitioners to fetch water for my needs. Sometimes, they would let women and children fetch water before inkomoti began.

Although Nyamihana's water pump was a place where people competed, I grew up in an environment that was supportive and encouraging. We were close friends and shared time together. We used to sing Dore Umunyanawee... together at weddings and religious events like baptisms. We shared many moments because we lived close to one another. My uncles Karemera Dominiko and John, Callixte Ndangurura and Ndamage Jules were my closest relatives. They were also my cousin Uwamaliya Renatha and her husband Habarugira. They were my childhood friends. We shared many happy times together, often gathering at their house or mine almost every day after playtime.

My happiest moments as a child were those days spent playing with my cousins Nyiranuma, Burandine, and those nights at Uncle Karemera's house, near ours, where I spent my nights. My cousins and I enjoyed laughing, playing, and eating together.

Memories of my childhood are Shimwa Claude, Gloriose, and talking to my cousins Rukara Rukara Gaudence, Gaudence, Fils Karemera. Locadiya was an elderly lady who lived near my house. I visited her often. I usually went there either in the morning or evening. She was always there for me, and was very kind. She used to say "Umugabo wanjie yaje" when I was with them, which meant "my husband has arrived". She was always willing to answer all my questions, and I got the chance ask many more. I was very curious! We laughed a lot together, and I always thought of her as my second mother.

When I think back to my childhood friends, we have lost the unity and happiness that marked our past. They were my family before that. Although I couldn't mention everyone, this memoir would not have been possible without the names that I have given. This memoir is essentially the story of the people I lived with and the story of our lives. Our lives were a testament to the strength of our parents, who deported to live in a country where there was no hope. Their hope has stayed with my throughout all of this.

3 NYIRARUKOBWA

My mother began telling me at six years old that I would be going to school the next year. Children started school at age seven because there were not many schools or kindergartens. I was excited and couldn't wait to go. I began telling everyone that Nyirarukobwa was where I was supposed go, a school built in 1960s in the Nyirarukobwa swamp between the hills of Kayumba and Kabaha, Karambi, Nyamabuye. On my way to Nyamihana's water pump, I used to pass Nyirarukobwa. The building fascinated me and I wondered when it would be time for me to go to school.

My mother's songs about school were what motivated me most. It was the best time a child can imagine singing together. I remember the song she taught me, which I sang on my way to school: "ku nzira-igaana, ku ishuli. ku inzira-igana.ku ishuli..." This song is still etched in my memory. Callixte, Karemera and Kabanda's kids were all already attending Nyirarukobwa Prima School. I would only see them on weekends.

My mum and I went to Kurarete Centre the day before we started school to purchase a small blackboard, crayons, and a pencil. These were what children used from Years One through Three before they could use textbooks. My mum returned from the trip to cook our dinner. My dad wasn't yet at home. Mum forced me to sit in the small living room. I was asked to rewrite the numbers 1-10 she had written on my blackboard.

"I can do it; I can do it!" My mind whispered to me.

After some time, mum came back. "Well, it's obvious that you are doing well. Keep going. You can erase those numbers and begin again! They were hard to erase, so I hesitated.

She insisted. She insisted.

That was all I did until my dad returned home. We had dinner. It felt like a long night because I was eager to get to school. It was finally the morning of September 1, 1991. My mother woke up very early to get me up.

"Today school starts!" She said.

 It was a great feeling to be able to leave my house.

"Mwaramutse!" (Morning!) My mom kept greeting people as we walked to school.

We passed through Nyirarukobwa, brightened by the rising sun's rays that pierced through the clouds. Some people were awake and cultivating their land, while others were already singing.

After passing Kwa Nyamamihana, we finally reached Nyirarukobwa school. I was happy, but also scared by the number of children screaming and playing.

Some of the boys were wearing khaki uniforms and were playing karere. They kicked the ball in various directions. There were several teams playing simultaneously within the school compound. While others were running after one another, some girls wearing contoni (a blue outfit for girls) were playing kudomana. It was an incredible moment! My mum was waiting impatiently for me to join them. My mum, surrounded by children and parents who had accompanied them to school for the first day, went to Mukunzi's class to inquire about Uwamaliya's classroom.

Mwalimu Mukunzi, Kanimba and mum talked to me, and we went to Uwamaliya Renatha's first-year classrooms. These were made out of wood, concrete, and mud. Nyirarukobwa School was a rectangular structure with a flagpole at the center. The southern section of the football fields was located near the swamp on the side Karambi hill. Many children from our village had been served by the school. To reach Uwamaliya's class, Mum and I had to walk through the densely packed compound. Many parents had already arrived to register their children. Uwamaliya called me after a while: "Omar Ndizeye " I didn't respond because my family used to call me Kaunda. This nickname was given to me by my father Kenneth Kaunda who visited Rwanda at the same time as I was born. She started to laugh after calling my name twice.

"Don't know your name?" She asked.

Finally, she registered me in the cahier de l'appel (a log that teachers use to record students present and absent). Then I returned home with my mom.

Nyirarukobwa was for me more than just a school, it was almost like my family. My cousins all studied there. Uwamaliya, my teacher, was also my sister's cousin. Kaboyi and Dominiko Karemera were my uncles. It made me feel like I was always there for my family by being with them at school. They were also great teachers. We felt like our parents. After their deportation from Bugesera, most of them had lived in Nyamata refugee camps. Some were deported, like my father from Ruhengeri in the Bukonya area. Mwalimu Kaboyi, the teacher, used to listen to Radio Rwanda from under a large tree. I remember vividly the passion that Nyirarukobwa teachers had for their jobs.

Playtime was my favorite moment at Nyirarukobwa School. It was when I spent time with my classmates Ngizwenayo, Fillete and Bingwa. They were my best friends in school. We would slide and slide in the mud when we returned home from school during the rainy season. It was scary but also very entertaining to watch. Others would chat or play Banana Football. We had no other choice but to play.

From my first year at school, Nyirarukobwa was an important part of my daily life until the genocide. The school was small and had no fancy buildings but it was connected to a community. It was a symbol for triumph over Nyamata's deportation of my people in the 1960s. Also, it helped to integrate deported Tutsi into their native community of Bugesera. On the way home from school, children had to colour the hills around Nyirarukobwa with blue and khaki, which were the colours of our uniforms.

4 THE PERSECUTION OF 1990S

Most Tutsis, particularly intellectuals, were arrested and taken to former commune offices when the war between RPF1 (the government of Habyarimana) began in 1990. Some were executed, while others were placed in stadiums throughout Rwanda. Bugesera was no exception. It was one of the most targeted areas. Things were only getting worse every day.

CDR3 and MRND2 members held political rallies in Bugesera. This created chaos. To mobilize their members, other political parties like PSD6 and PL4 MDR5 were also holding rallies in Bugesera. They came in large numbers. Extremist members would climb onto their cars roofs. CDR and MRND members decimated shops in Kurarete and beat up Kurarete residents. This was the most violent incident I can remember. They stole merchandise and broke into homes in the centre. The Tutsis of Bugesera were also attacked shortly before the genocide. Some fled to Nyamata while others were burned to their homes. Refugees arrived from the hills of Nyamabuye and Karambi, as well as other parts of Bugesera. My parents began to think about moving during the worst time of 1992, even though the attacks hadn't reached our area. Although it was a difficult time, we weren't harassed at school by Tutsis from other areas of Rwanda. This was due to the fact that most of our teachers were Tutsis. The killings, displacements and closings of schools were all things that I thought about. It was a nightmare to think of the Tutsi massacre in Bugesera in 1992. It was difficult to put into words the terrible time in my life when everything seemed uncertain. I was a child who longed for a bright future. It was hard to accept this reality.

Tensions grew, and Nyirarukobwa saw a steady stream of political parties rallying. Teaching continued as normal, but with occasional interruptions. One day, a long parade of soldiers passed our school and went into the swamp. We were thrilled to see them, as it was something that was not common. Although I tried to listen, I couldn't help but look outside.

We all ran to Nyirarukobwa during the break and saw a military helicopter low over the swamp. Everyone was excited and shouting. This was the first helicopter that I had ever seen. The soldiers returned to their positions in the evening. We didn't know what their mission was. It got worse. The inkomoti at Nyamihana's water pump were more violent than usual, but it was difficult for us children to understand what was going on. It was difficult to live in, and it was also difficult to describe. Soldiers were not only seen in large numbers but also some of their neighbours, such as teacher Murangwa's children. In 1992, they were killed in Gikondo (a Kigali area). The whole school was afraid when their bodies were returned to their village for burial.

Because most of my neighbors were Tutsis deported from Ruhengeri, or native of Bugesera, Interahamwe militia wasn't common in the area I was born. They were also known as Abamere. They had trained Interahamwe in the nearby areas. Kamaka, who lived in Nyamabuye, was the most well-known. One day, I was surprised to see a young man in an Interahamwe uniform, with green, red, and black, at Nyamihana's water pump. It was quite scary to see. It was terrifying to see!

1994 was my third year in primary school. Our Easter holidays began in a strange mood. The end of term ceremony for primary school students was to be held in the football field in the presence our parents. However, this year there were fewer family members present and the ceremony took places near the Rwandan flag which is located in front of the primary school buildings. One teacher read out the names of the five first pupils in our class. My heart began to pound when my teacher started reading. My name was read second by my close friend Ngizwenayo. He had fled the 1992 Bagogwe massacres with his parents. They fled the massacres to Narcisse's home. Third was my niece Fiette, who is the daughter of Uwamaliya. This made me very happy and I didn't follow the rest of my names because of it. The fear that I felt as my teacher began reading the names made me sweat. My parents weren't there to meet me in class, which was one side of my problem. However, I was excited for the next term. It was not known that this would be our last term.

You ask questions as a child. My question was "Why are these things happening?" I had heard of the many killings on the news and listened to the radio with my dad. Fear had taken over my thoughts and I kept wondering what would happen if they attacked us. I imagined I could hide under the bed of my parents, and no one would find it. These thoughts were childish daydreams.

Sibomana was a son Lokadiya's, the elderly lady who lived next to us. He bought newspapers including Kangura and Kanguka. I loved sitting in their tiny sitting room, reading through the newspapers from the first page to the last. But the more I read, the more scared I became. The majority of articles were about the fighting between President Habyarimana and the RPF Inkotanyi. Others were more extreme, and they followed the ten Hutu commands. The most frightening articles were published in Kangura, December 1990.

Although I enjoyed practicing my reading skills, I returned home with many questions and wondered why there was so much hatred toward Tutsis. I didn't understand enough to be able to comprehend everything, so I soon returned to playing with my peers.

5 HABYARIMANA HAS DIED!

April is a month that rains in Rwanda. It also means April in Kinyarwanda, which literally means "a month of milk." April 1994 began with mixed emotions. I had just finished my second term in my third year, with excellent grades. Everywhere crops were growing well. That was amazing! Mum was still suffering from severe malaria at home. My father decided to send my mother to Kigali to get medical treatment after a long night of sleepless nights. My father was the older child and I agreed to stay with him to take care of my younger brother Mpayimana Rashidkawawa. My father decided Nyampinga Farida (my younger sister) should go with mum. They left in the early hours of March 1994. It was very worrying to see my mother so sick. She was attacked by Interahamwe militia members the last time she visited Kigali. This was because Nyinawumwami (Kinyarwanda) means "the mother-of-the King". I did my chores at home and fetched water. Although I don't know why, I was worried.

After almost two weeks, I started missing mum deeply. Because my dad didn't have any contact information, I was unable to ask him for news. The only way to get in touch with him was to wait for someone to return from Kigali. Mukiza, Kabanda's son, came out of a taxi to meet me on my way to the centre. Mukiza had traveled to Kigali to see Kabanguka's relatives. Kabanguka was a member of his family. Annisia, Kabanguka's wife and their two sons stayed at the Rubirizi training centre Kabanguka ran.

"Have you seen my mum?" He asked me with a heavy heart.

"Yes, I saw her. She is doing great!" She said she would be back before Easter. He replied.

I thought to myself, "Oh, how the days don't go by quickly enough", but I was so happy she was doing well.

I waited impatiently for my stepmother to return from Kigali, where she was still staying at Rubirizi's house.

My father cooked dinner on April 6th. After dinner, my younger brother and me went to bed. My father could not sleep without the news. He was tired that night and didn't turn on Radio Rwanda or Muhabura. This is the RPF radio station that most people in the area listen to. Inkotanyi's news was missed.

My cousin Anastase, Marcel and Venant Bihusi, my cousin, had also joined them along with Narcisse and other neighbors. Narcisse's wife, Narcisse, had traveled to Kinihira with her husband to see him at the RPF headquarter. She returned with many exciting stories. She spoke about how men were happy to see her, but that discipline was extremely strict. All of them dreamed about Inkotanyi some day. It could bring an end to their long marginalization. Their hopeless existence of educating their children at secondary school level would mean they had to send them to Zaire. Kabanguka, our distant cousin, had been there. Dominiko, our uncle, used to visit him in Congo. Radio Muhabura was very popular during that time in our neighborhood.

My father got up early the next morning, April 7, 1994 to sell his crops to Kigali residents. As usual, Nyamihana's water pump was my first stop. I decided to fill two jerrycans with a smaller can. My dad was looking for help in making banana juice. I went into his room while he was busy in the banana field. I thought, "Wow! Now I can just listen to the radio!" When I turned the dial, classical music was playing. Radio Rwanda was the only option I had, as Radio Muhabura transmits in the afternoon. I waited for a while and then I heard an announcement: a journalist had reported that President Habyarimana died in a plane accident the night before. My heart started pounding. I wanted to be the one to tell my dad. I ran to the banana fields.

"Papa, Papa, Papa... Habyarimana yapfuye! "Habyarimana has passed away!" "Where did that come from?" He asked.

"The radio," I answered.

"Turashize! (We are done! He said to the men on the field, "We are done!" "Bring the radio to this place."

I returned home with his radio. Every few minutes, the announcement was broadcast along with a reminder asking people to remain at their homes. My father and the others began to discuss the 1960s and what they had experienced. Callixte was born in the interim.

"Wamenye Ko Ikinani Cyapfuye"

Everyone seemed worried. The neighborhood was quiet and there was less movement than usual. Each person had their own opinion. I took the jerrycans and went to Nyamihana's water pump.

Three people were discussing Habyarimana's death while I was on my way. Everyone was anxious about what would happen. Radio Rwanda had advised people not to leave their homes and not to gather in groups, but there was not enough danger to make people afraid to meet in our neighborhood: neither Interahamwe Hutu militia nor government soldiers were present. Things got worse in the afternoon. It rained first, then it was very distant from us, and we could see houses being set on fire in the hills. On the way to Nyamata, refugees began to appear. Rumours began to spread. We learned how the attacks started at Kanzenze under the command of the notorious Kamaka. It was terrible! Everyone was afraid.

My father was there to comfort me. Every child sees his dad as a hero, and that was what I felt.

The situation got worse on the second day of April 8, when Radio Rwanda announced the deaths one after another. Fighting broke out in Nyamabuye between Interahamwe, led by Kamaka, and the Tutsi resistance. My father sent us to Dominiko, his older brother. We joined the resistance with many of our neighbors. People were fleeing. My brother Rashid Kawawa, and I, were staying at Gloriose.

Claude Shimwa with Petero, my uncle Dominiko's children. It was hilarious to see Gloriose singing "RPF ganzaa", the RPF song. They couldn't stop laughing and were so happy.

Papa and the other men returned from Nyamabuye in the evening. Rukara, Domoniko's cousin, had fallen and injured his shoulder. Dominiko was the most well-respected man in our community. He was a Nyirarukobwa senior teacher and a Kanzenze Catholic Parish catechist. Dominiko was able to hear the men tell Dominiko about their experiences fighting the Interahamwe. My father finally decided to bring us home. I was extremely worried. I didn't know what had happened my mother, and the stories I heard at Domoniko's house scared me.

We sat silently on the way back. My father carried my little brother on his shoulders. We got home and immediately went to bed. It was hard for me to imagine what my father had done. My dad took me back to Domoniko's home after I fell asleep.

He said, confidently, "Mugende Musigare kwa Dominiko Turasubira Nimugoroba" My father was trying to encourage us, he knew it wasn't an easy fight. Some Interahamwe were being taken to the commune by government gendarmes. He saw Dominiko's injuries and had witnessed some Tutsis being murdered. Nearly every neighboring house was housing refugees from Nyamabuye's hills. Our world was filled with silence and questions about the future.

6 GOING TO KARAMBI HILL

My father took my younger brother and me to Domoniko's home again on the third day of April, 10th. He returned home and was ready to fight the Interahamwe. He was gone for the entire day. Rumours began to spread that we were being attacked. Yozefa, Dominiko's spouse, and some of their children began packing. We ran in the direction Kurarete. We stopped at Kanobana's house. Kanobana, a neighbor living just a few meters from Dominiko's home, was also there. We stayed there for a while, but only had a few seconds to decide if we wanted to return or go on. We were children and believed no one could touch our bodies because our parents were there. I imagined that if the Interahamwe attacked me, I would hide under the bed so no one could find me. These childhood dreams began to fade when Yozefa, and other elderly people became terrified. They were reminiscing about the 1960s. We were innocent children and couldn't understand the situation, but we could see everything in their eyes. It was terrible. Kanobana was our host.

The Tutsi refugee numbers had begun to decrease on the way to Nyamata. However, some were still fleeing Kanzenze and Nyamabuye towards Nyamata while others headed to Ntarama Catholic Church. Since 1959, Tutsis have sought refuge in churches. My parents, grandparents and other relatives were among those who were deported from Bugesera. They remembered how Janja Catholic Mission was their first refuge after fleeing to Ndusu. Then they were taken to Ruhengeri. Because her father was in prison early in 1963, my mother's parents didn't have this chance.

My father returned in the evening and began telling Dominiko about how the attacks were getting more severe. He suggested that they leave their home but Dominiko refused to agree. He believed that they would not do anything even if they got to him. After having baptized many Hutu kids at Kanzenze Catholic Parish, and many at Nyirarukobwa primary school, he was familiar with their needs.

My father decided to not take us home that evening and instead flee to Karambi Hill, which is located between Nyamata's school Nyirarukobwa. Dominiko's house was dark and we had only the moonlight as our guide. My father carried Kawawa with him on his shoulders and I was in his arms as we walked along the narrow path to Nyirarukobwa. We arrived at the school, passed through our classrooms, then went through the Nyirarukobwa swamp jumping over small streams and the mud. My long-suffering dad, who had suffered atrocities from his childhood, was the only thing I could picture. The sound of his heart breaking in the swamp was a reminder of the mountain of painful memories that he had. We crossed the swamp and climbed up the hill, passing through sorghum fields to reach Anakeleti's house. Anakeleti was Callixte's brother. The area was still without electricity and phones at the time. We were surprised to find another family of refugees there when we arrived. We slept on the ground for the night.

Anakeleti began milking his cows the next morning when we woke up. My father returned home. Everything was gone. His brothers Callixte and Dominiko, his sisters Kabanda and Sole, were still living in their homes with their families. After I had drunk milk, my brother and I began walking with Anakeleti, our classmates Sole, and her younger brother. We ran around the field next to Anakeleti's house. We were so innocent! Every child is an angel. How did we forget all the dangers that we faced before we arrived there? My father was supposed to come home and take us home, or even live with us. My mind drifted to Anakeleti's comfort, and I almost forgot about my mother, who was still living in Kigali. I believed that there would be no Interahamwe Hutu militia attacking us in this house. It was childish! Anakeleti decided to join us near the Kayumba forest, so we didn't spend the night there. Kayumba was the scene of many refugees. My younger brother Kawawa was still with me. The first time we entered a house was near Kariyeri, on Kayumba hill. My father was still not there. As night approached, I began to worry. My father was not being seen by the Tutsis, although they were still coming. As my younger brother Kawawa asked me where Dad was, I felt pain. "He will come," I told him repeatedly.

I asked everyone around, but there was still no news about my father. I began to cry, believing he had been murdered. I wondered how I would spend my remaining years with my brother. I realized that the night before in Nyirarukobwa's swamps was not our last, but only the beginning of many more. With throngs of Tutsis displaced, and children crying, I heard my father's voice calling me in the darkness!

"Kaunda? Kaunda?"

"Yes, I'm here!" I finally hugged him again, and my tears turned to joy.

My father brought my younger brother with him and we sat together in the sitting room. He was alive and present, which made me very happy. He shared with us his struggles with Kabanda, Callixte and himself. All was going well until Interahamwe entrapped them in Nyirarukobwa's swamp. My heart was racing, but I managed not to let it get out of my chest! Although it was only a story, I still felt the danger. My father had spent nearly two hours hiding in the sorrow. Callixte, Kabanda and he lost touch with each other. They all met up again at the last minute, and then they climbed Kayumba's hill. My father began to inquire about Anakeleti, as he had forgotten us at Anakeleti's house. He was happy, but also very upset when he saw us. We shared the night together, old people sharing stories in the house, outside, and in neighboring houses. All of us were refugees, children, and seniors, and shared the same rooms and compound. Although I can't recall how we ate, it is likely that someone cooked for us. I fell asleep in that crowd and woke up the next day not knowing what to do.

All of Kayumba's forest was filled with Tutsi refugees. We set out for the hill. We passed Callixte, Kabanda and my dad's place of refuge, which was in a small bush next to the path. We continued our journey to the forest, where they took some tools with us. It was nearly 8 AM when we reached the forest. Maliya began to shuck beans for cooking. Many Tutsi refugees were also doing the same. Everybody was busy, some making food, while others were trying to build a burende (a small, grass-covered house). Kabanda, Callixte and my father set out to build a house together. My younger brother kept calling my dad and he continued to go. Things got worse at 10 AM. We started hearing gunshots. My younger brother and I were taken by my father. The forest was surrounded by soldiers who were firing wildly. Nobody knew where to hide, or how to run. We followed their lead and tried to stop them from reaching Nyamata.

We thought we were going to die, but there was no way out. The soldiers were the only way to Nyamata and out of the forest. Nyamata was dead. We could see smoke from burning houses and hear gunshots coming from the town. My father was still there. We lost Kawawa in the retreat of hundreds upon hundreds of hunted human like us. They gathered in many different groups, each trying to get as far as possible away from the gunshots. My father and me joined one of these groups. We headed together to Nyamata's slaughterhouse to get to the Nyamata Muslim Mosque. After passing through a narrow street near the mosque, we finally arrived at Nyamata football field. It took us more than two hours to reach Nyamata. On the way, several people were killed, including Anakeleti's wife who was shot just before we reached Nyamata. I didn't understand what was happening.

The football field was filled with government soldiers armed with guns. We formed a small group and squeezed ourselves until we ran out of oxygen. God bless a mysterious hero to whom my dad turned for a taste the banana juice he had in salabash. I would have died without that man and his juice. May God bless him with a beautiful spot in heaven, regardless of whether he died or is still living. He saved me, my father and I, and had the courage to reach out at the most crucial moment. We saw terrible things in front of the Kanzenze commune offices. There were soldiers raiding small neighborhoods of Kajevuba, Gatare. We all could see our days were over. If we had days, it might only take a few hours. Two soldiers came across a man in a shop near Gatare. He was violently pulled out by the soldiers who beat him with a wood club until he died. The body of the victim lay there for over an hour before militia arrived and took him away. I'm not sure if his body was thrown away, or buried. It was shocking to me that things could get so horrendous. Every minute was our last chance to live on this planet.

The devil's terrors continued to amaze us in that frightening moment. Two Daihatsu minibuses carrying Interahamwe Hutu militias suddenly passed us. They were singing "Eeh Tubatsembatsembe" ("Let's exterminate them!"). We were still being surrounded by government soldiers, who kept us locked in a small area. Because the soldiers were still firing at houses around us, some were sat on the legs and others. The Interahamwe, two Daihatsus, quickly surrounded the entire area. As if that wasn't enough, we also saw behind us a Mercedes Benz army truck with men armed in machetes.

We were able to take a break from the scorching midday sun as evening approached. We were forced to sit together in front of the commune. Some even trampling each other. The Bourgmestre of Gatanazi was standing next to a flag when we saw him. We all began to believe he was going out to save us. "Why aren't you here?" Leave! You are right in front of my office. Mujye padiri (Go see the priest). His tone was arrogant. He believed he was God and could end our lives at any moment. We ran together towards the Nyamata Catholic Church. Callixte, Maliya and I remained with each other. Maliya took my hands. We passed through Nyamata's primary school compound. It was a narrow passage between the classrooms, and the school toilets. Surviving was hard work. I was scared, hungry, and tired. Others were shouting. We had to get to the church, and there was no time for us to think about ourselves.

As the doors weren't completely closed, I accidentally stepped inside the toilets when we got there. The shocking face of a man wearing red eyes caught my attention. The Interahamwe Hutu militias were already surrounding us. We increased our speed. Maliya held my hand, but it was difficult to keep the group together in that crowd. The Interahamwe Hutu militias seemed to want to surround us and finish us off. We reached a narrow street that ran between Nun's house, the stables at Locatelli. I turned my attention towards the school. Interahamwe was surrounding us. They began to come towards us with their whistles. I let go Maliya's hands and ran, pushing through the crowd. This was a fight for survival, as she was not running fast enough.

We finally reached the church. After a few minutes, Maliya, Callixte, and my dad found me. As the church was full, others went to the Sunday school located on the opposite side of the convent. Many children were crying, and everyone was talking with their neighbors, spouses, or husbands. It was difficult to forget that night in the church because of the noise and the stuffy atmosphere.

To Callixte and Maliya, Maliya said "Ubwo towageze mu ikiliziya nutacyo tutukibaye" (Now that we're in the church nothing will happen), She was referring back to years past, when Tutsis fled to the church to find safety. It saved them during those years in the 1960s and 1992.

I wish someone had told us this was different.

7 EPHEMERAL HOPE

Although I felt comforted by the number of people in the church the next morning, it was also the second day without food, and it was very painful. We felt dizzy when we woke up and decided to go outside. Callixte, my dad and other men had been to the convent. I was left behind with Maliya, and was devastated by Kawawa's disappearance. He was probably killed along the way.

My dad returned with Callixte later in the morning. They had prepared porridge and rice. Maliya, Maliya, and I were sitting near Locatelli's grave next to the church when we saw them. Because I was hungry, I felt a bit happier. While they were cooking, Mukanoheli came from Nyamata Primary School's street. Mignone was little on her back. Mignone was Theophile's firstborn daughter. Mukanoheli was also leading the Kawawa by his hand! It was so wonderful to be back together. God saved their lives! Mukanoheli shared with us their night spent in a bush. Mignone kept asking Kawawa where her grandmother was. Everyone laughed when we heard the story. But in her innocence she was correct; she didn't know that certain people she knew had been killed.

While Maliya was walking around the compound, Maliya began to cook porridge and rice. Anakeleti's daughter, Sole, was sitting on the balcony with her father and younger brother. She was grieving for her mother, who died on the way to Nyamata. We couldn't help her. I looked at her with fear and emotion. I was afraid that the same thing could happen to myself. Finally, the food was ready. Even though it was just boiled rice, it was delicious and we enjoyed every bite. We sat down next to Locatelli's grave and another priest who had been killed in Rwanda during Pope John Paul II's early 1990s visit.

The cemetery was located at the back of Nyamata Catholic Parish. It contained the priests' houses, the nuns cloister, and Sunday schools. While we were there, Tutsi refugees continued to arrive from the hills of Maranyundo and Mayange, Kayumba and Musenyi, as well as other parts around Nyamata. They came with their cows, and other property. They arrived in large numbers, both young and old. Nyamata was a mixture of people and animals. It was a very distressing situation. It was a distressing situation?

Although the first day was calm, the fear of death persisted throughout the day. Hunger was the worst part. We had food but could not eat another meal.

Maliya and Kawawa were sitting with me on the fence of Locatelli's nuns' cloister. Someone had brought us sorghum porridge with no sugar. Mignone refused to eat it and continued crying. Kawawa and me remained calm and had some. As a Rwandan would call it, "haryoha inzara". No matter what the taste, you will eat whatever you like.

We were forced to endure the heat and cows of those hot sunny days. Our parents were already looking sad and could not have asked for more. Although the end of the first day didn't promise much hope it wasn't that scary. We returned to the church. We children slept on the legs and backs of our parents in the heat, surrounded by crying babies and refugees who wailed about their fate. That evening, we had no food. I can tell you that my cries were muted by sadness, uncertainty about the future and hunger. So I fell asleep in the dark church of Nyamata.

The second day at church began as the first, with a line of military trucks suddenly appearing in the compound. White soldiers! White soldiers!

Maliya said, "They are coming for us to protect them, I tell you." We were all very happy to have them there, as we had been subject to minor attacks from Interahamwe from the cemetery side.

Some soldiers were munching on biscuits and chewing gum while they were at the top of their tanks. A few even gave some biscuits to children in the vicinity. We saw white priests and nuns coming out of the monastery and convent. Some of their goods were being loaded into the trucks by them. We were not able to see the trucks with the nuns and white priests. We understood that protection of the Tutsis fleeing Nyamata Church and the surrounding areas, which number more than 10,000, was not the concern for the French or Belgian soldiers. They were there to save their fellows.

Maliya, Maliya, and I went to Anakeleti's Sunday School in the afternoon. The church was suddenly attacked by gunfire and Interahamwe spears, arrows. They tried to weaken the Tutsi resistance, but they were defeated with stones.

The Interahamwe arrived in large numbers this time, but they were unable to get into the Sunday Schools. Children, elderly, and women in fear were hiding in the church and convent. Because of the gunshots, people were laying down. I was able to raise my head and see through the window that a group of Interahamwe, some old men, were attacking the side of compound just in front of the church. The resistance held them back from all sides. In the exchange of stones against gunfire and spears, arrows, some cows were killed. Finally, Interahamwe surrendered and fled. We left Sunday School after the attack.

Kawawa and my dad were present in the church, so I was concerned and wanted to find them. We saw the bodies of some Tutsis who were injured and also those from cows that had been killed. Later, those cows were served as food. The church was our home for the night. Although there were no attacks the next day, it was obvious that our days were over.

8 A NIGHTMARE IN THE CHURCH OF NYAMATA

The morning of April 15th was beautiful, sunny, and filled with fresh air. It was a wonderful day. Because of the previous attack, all refugees had woken early to get ready for work. The compound was full of children, while adults were seated and discussing in small groups. It was dangerous to move from the area. A soldier riding a motorcycle stopped by the church to take a look, and then he left just as quickly as he arrived. The situation was calm. As the hours went by, it became more hot.

We all fled the church from fear when some refugees ran around 3pm. "Interahamwe have arrived!" Old and young men went out to fight back using stones and other materials. They were fighting for their survival against highly-trained, heavily-armed government soldiers. Some Tutsis who were resisting the government soldiers were killed. Others fled to the church after seeing the Interahamwe. It was hell on Earth: Children, elders and women, all saw death coming. Although the fighters shut down the doors to the church, it did not stop soldiers from firing their bullets. They then threw grenades in a packed church. The blasts and women's desperate prayers lost me.

Our last hope in this fight to death was to pray to God to give us a new life in heaven. It seemed like we were getting close to our final day. I realized that I wouldn't cry even if it meant I was going to be dead. I would be strong.

Is there another option? My soul was in pain and I wanted to comfort it. My dad and the other men, both young and old, continued to throw stones, shoes, and any other items they could find in an attempt to stop the soldiers from entering the church. I was sitting on the bench near the metal pillar at the west end of the church. My father, still having some money, pulled out a 100-franc note and gave it to him. "Uzabe umugabo!" (Be strong! He said.

It was only a matter time, not hours. Kawawa was still present in the church crowd. The strategy adopted by the Tutsi fighters was to throw whatever they could, then lie down to avoid being hit with bullets.

Many died from the grenades thrown into the church, as well as the bullets fired by a sniper from behind the altar with his AK47. He silenced the prayers, the cries of the children and the screams from the injured, as well as the cries of the people praying. The church was now filled with blood, as dead and living bodies were mixed on the floor.

The killings stopped after a series of intense explosions and rounds de gunfire. There was no resistance. The injured took their last breaths. It was chaos. As I looked out, hundreds of Interahamwe militiamen sat in line in front of the church wearing banana leaves. They had returned in large numbers, armed with spears, machetes, wooden clubs and other weapons. We thought they had vanished. A small object was being thrown into the church from near me. It started to emit smoke after a few seconds. It was a tear gas canister, and it filled the entire church with white smoke. This made our eyes and nostrils burn. It was impossible to see my friends and family, and it made breathing difficult.

I've never experienced so much pain as those moments in the smoke. I thought I would die from asphyxiation. It dispersed and I felt like I was in heaven. I began to hallucinate from the lack of oxygen. The look on the faces of those still alive was so startling that I can't even describe it. All eyes were red from the gas and they all thought about how painfully they were about dying.

My father was the only one I could see. I could see the sorrow in his eyes, and the terror when Callixte raised up to throw his last shoe. He fell to the ground as if he was suddenly asleep. Maliya called my father and asked him to wake him.

My father said to her, "He is dead." They had no time to grieve because the first soldier entered the church in that instant. I will always remember the image of an elderly man holding a machete and trying to fight back the soldier. That soldier killed him because he was the last of the resistance. As Hutu militiamen entered the church, I was forced to hide under a bench. They loved killing and competing as if it were a game. The sounds of the wooden clubs were very clear to me. It was odd to think that many of them had been baptized in this exact church. They were ruthless because they saw themselves as Tutsis, crushing their heads like snakes or cockroaches and singing their song "Eeh Tubatsembatsembe".

Slowly, the Interahamwe came closer to me under the bench. I lay in the blood from the bodies of the people around me that had been cut up. While some of them were beating people to death, others were cutting them up with machetes. They were removing the bodies of those who were hiding beneath them and began to kill them. They started to pile dead bodies on top of me in the chaos. I was starving! They eventually saw me but couldn't take me. Instead, they beat my legs. I didn't cry or move. They might have thought that I was dead, like the rest. Thank goodness I kept my word to myself. They continued the massacre and moved on. Some children were near the altar when I heard the last Tutsi voice. One was calling Jesus, the other was shouting the Hallelujah. Both were also silenced in a matter of seconds. The church was very quiet.

Interahamwe were the only remaining voices. They sang their opposition chants back to the dying, mocking them. They told the dead, "Wake up and sing!" Some murderers were near me, searching for bodies to make money. They stole the 100 francs that my father gave me. They valued the money more than their lives. Two militiamen began quarrelling about a bag that one of them had taken off a corpse. They continued their argument and ran out of church.

At 6 p.m., no voices could be heard. I finally raised my head. I was in the middle small piles of bodies. Maliya was the first person I saw. There was blood everywhere, and she was sat between two benches. Maliya recognised me as I was removing myself from the bodies. She was shaking, taking her last breaths. "Can you give my water?" she asked. But I couldn't move because my legs were hurt. As I approached her, it became clear why Interahamwe had not saved her life: a part of her shoulder was blown away by the grenade, and her head was severely injured. She was in her final minutes. As she told me she was thirsty, I wondered what I could do. I then saw others who had survived. One of Mukurarinda's daughters was the one I recognized. Mukurarinda was my cousin Uwamaliya's brother, Habarugira.

"Could you please help Maliya?" Please. Please, she needs water! Others were also moving from underneath the benches. Some were hurt. They tried to take Maliya out, but she died before they could get her outside. I stayed, searching for my father. He was not among the survivors. I saw his body, lying on top of the pile of bodies. I turned his head. I saw blood pouring from his nose. A machete had broken his backbone. I turned him over. I didn't cry for my father, I knew that I would. I pray that God will grant him his soul. I went without meeting Kawawa. Locatelli's grave is the last picture I have of him. It will always be in my mind forever. I was lost in the darkness. The walls and roof of the church were covered in blood. Grenades had ripped holes in the walls. My father was gone. I left Kawawa Callixte and Maliya. I didn't leave to live, but to continue to struggle.

I wasn't sure if I would make it through that night or the next day.

It was dark when I left the church. My body was covered in blood, as were my clothes. My legs were beaten by militia men to see if they could still kill me. I was now hobbling. I didn't have anywhere to go but the survivors were headed to the convent just a few meters from the church. Everyone was climbing up the fence because the Tutsis had opened the gate for them. That was impossible with my legs. I then saw Karimunda (whom we used to call Pusi). He was Maliya Muzayirwa's grandson, and our neighbor. Pusi was in the convent when he saw me and called "Kaunda!" You can climb to get here.

"I can't, because my legs are hurt," I responded.

He pulled me up on the fence, then he went back in and lifted me off the fence onto the ground. I was exhausted, in shock, and very hungry. Pusi was from the church, where his father and mine had been murdered. Because it was the only food left, people were cooking the carcasses of the cows that had been killed in the attack.

We all shared the food when it was ready. But I couldn't eat any of it because my mind was elsewhere. The events were being discussed in groups. They were envious of us and wanted to do everything they could to help. We fell asleep eventually.

The convent continued to function the next morning, April 16, 1994. Everyone was still shocked when we woke up. I didn't know where to go or how to escape the shock of seeing my father dead. He was not the only one who died in the church. It was also the case of thousands of Tutsis. Anakeleti was my spiritual home in the convent. His daughter Sole, his last-born child, and his son were still with him. I could hear children playing outside the church. But I didn't want to go back to the darkness in the interior. I was able to forget the terrible experience from the previous day. I was horrified at what had happened to me as a ten-year old. I was constantly wondering how my life could become life again. They served me lunch, but I couldn't eat. Fearful and anxious, my mind was not yet in control. We heard sounds outside the church's fence at 2 p.m. Interahamwe was back, likely to kill the children who were playing near the church. As Interahamwe began shouting and singing as they dismantled the fence, I realized that this was going to be my final day. They arrived earlier than usual and were accompanied by soldiers of Gako military camp.

Anakeleti, terrified, took Sole and his son to a small field near the priest's house. They followed me. He asked us to lay down on the ground and put banana leaves over us, but I hesitated because it was in plain view of the Hutu militiamen who were shouting "Erega Muzehe nushaka tubice hakiri, kare, ntaho muducikira!" The soldiers were firing at our gates and throwing grenades as we ran out of time. We were witness to the apocalypse. Anakeleti was terrified and said, "Uratuma Bambonera Abana". We didn't have any other options, so I understood his fear. He saw death coming and had no way to protect his children. Death was coming from the Hutus outside of the gate.

They were singing again.

It was the end. We ran out of those banana leaves and went back to the priest's house veranda, but it was too late. The soldiers were already inside the compound. We laid down and placed ibibambano, traditional papyrus mats, over our heads. It was not a refuge, it was just a lie to our souls that it was. Truth was, life on Earth was becoming a terrible place. I couldn't hide anymore. The soldier who first reached the veranda first kicked the ibibambano. Fear fell on us all. He reached out to me and instructed the rest of the soldiers to follow his lead. They were led to a small area near the banana plantation. We followed the soldier, who held onto my hand. I felt paralysed. I wondered if this was my last chance to live on this planet. I looked at the AK47 of the soldier. He was a pityr in my eyes. I was in the clutches of a devil. We reached our next graveyard in less than one minute. The first victims were already broken up. There were also lines of Interahamwe who had been sent to kill Tutsis being brought in by soldiers.

The Tutsis were becoming more terrified by the day. Standing on a small gate, where soldiers and Interahamwe were passing through, I saw that Tutsis were being hidden in priests' homes. Anakeleti was wearing a black suit. Sole, her brother, and Sole were placed on the ground before us. Interahamwe began beating Anakeleti's heads with a wooden club. He exclaimed, "Hold on!" when the soldier raised the wooden clubs to beat him again. I will bring my son with me to the execution! I can't recall if my heart was still beating, or if it was already dead. The militia had already stopped beating Anakeleti before I was allowed to join them. Two Interahamwe had machetes in their arms and a pregnant woman, who was crying, arrived at her place. They were asked to spare her, as the Hutu child was in her womb.

"Don't worry. We are going to take the child. The soldiers assured him that he would live. They forced her to lie down next to Anakeleti. Sole and her brother were now silent. They died looking at their father, who was beating them to death. Anakeleti called me again, "My son come." We'll die together!"

"Go!" The soldier holding my hand said, "Go!"

He went and I hesitated. The Tutsis were the ones who wanted to beat the refugees with machetes and wooden clubs. I moved towards the crowd of desperate people, who were counting down their final moments on Earth. Everyone was afraid, and waited to die. The pregnant woman waited to be killed with the other Tutsis. I hid behind the crowd. Everyone was trying to get killed. I saw two daughters from Mukurarinda who had helped me take Maliya out the church.

Everyone was trying to hide behind that small house. As I tried to get away from the Tutsis group, I noticed a small step. "Let's try," I thought. I tried to climb it but I was too short and couldn't reach the top. Everyone was behind me waiting for me to climb up to their turn. I was unable to reach the top, my hands only touched the fence's top. I glanced behind me and saw Interahamwe approaching with a wooden club in his raised arm. I pushed and shoved until I fell like a tree over the fence. Because I had forgotten the real pain, I didn't feel any pain. Because it was the only way to escape death, my body was ready.

I was able to land in a large banana field. Although I thought I was just outside the fence, when I looked around, I saw that there was a larger fence surrounding the banana plantation. I noticed people slowly moving behind Abaseriziyani's house. "Those might have been Tutsis," I thought, but I decided to stay in the hole that I'd landed in. It was possibly used by nuns to plant banana trees and collect weeds.

It was terrifying to hear the gunshots and hear the screams from the victims behind the fence that I just climbed. I continued to watch the movements of those in the distance until I realized they were Tutsis, who had escaped the murder just like me. I moved out of the hole to join them. They had placed a tree in front of the fence so they could climb it when I got there. I failed twice on the climb. Then I remembered what I saw in the compound, and I tried harder to reach it. Finally, I made it! I then had to go over the other side.

It was done by others. One militiaman came out of the church carrying tools, jerry cans, and other belongings he had taken from murdered Tutsis. He saw us escaping. I ran straight towards the fence and jumped down. The man shouted, "Catch them!" He continued his journey. I finally got out of prison after climbing the fence of death.

9 A LOST BOY ON KAYUMBA HILL

We were four that evening, and two of us hid in a bush just a few meters from the Abaseriziyani fence. I and another young boy hid in a bush close to Abaseriziyani's fence. Two men in long coats were found there. They were scared to see us as they believed that the Interahamwe might have followed us. We explained to them that we had only seen one Interahamwe and that he had gone. We refused to move to another bush. We stayed and were bitten repeatedly by mosquitos. We could hear Interahamwe scream from Maranyundo's sides, just a few meters from Nyamata Church. They were likely chasing the last Tutsis hiding in houses or bushes.

The two men decided in the darkness to travel to Kigali. We asked them if we would go along, but they said no. We tried to convince the young boy and me that we could get to the city, but they refused. This was the first time I had ever been completely alone in my entire life. I kept asking them if they could show me the way to Kurarete. They could only go back to Kurarete, as that was the only place I knew. They finally agreed to do so. We followed them through the bush, knowing the area well. I was wearing a stained t-shirt and shorts from the church. It was extremely cold. The men advised us to follow the road to Kurarete, as we had previously agreed.

"This is the road to Nyamata. The opposite road leads to Kigali. They will take you to Kurarete," stated the men.

We couldn't choose and chose to travel to Kurarete while the men went to Kayumba. It was dark, we were hungry, tired and scared by the unknown. It was hard to believe that those two men didn't let us all go together. But they were trying to save our lives.

We were discussing the best route to Kariyeri (a center before Kurarete), a few meters down the road when we heard something that sounded like a set of drawn knives. "Muhagarare aho!" (Stop there!)

We were approaching a soldier. It was so dark that we hadn't seen him. I ran into the bushes near the road and hiding. While the soldier pursued him, the young man ran towards Nyamata. I thought, "I'm about dying." I stopped at a small tree in a bush next to the road. My heart was racing and I was short of breath. I ran to escape my second death, this time in darkness. I didn't know where I was or the way to get me back to Kurarete. I knew the place and the path, but I had no idea. I returned to the road to find my friend, and I headed back towards Nyamata. In the days and minutes to come, we were not sure what would happen to our lives. When I reached the area near ADPR where we had split from those men, it was already dark and I was hungry. I laid down on the grass next to a small bush. To escape the biting mosquitoes, I covered my head with the t-shirt. The blood smell was too strong for me to bear, so I chose to sleep with my hands in the t-shirt. Only through hunger, exhaustion, and sadness could I sleep. These mosquitoes were happy to see a young boy that they could bite and not move. I fell asleep like I was dead. I couldn't hear any sounds. I was in a different world to the one where all my family members had died. I was the only survivor and a young boy in desperate need.

It was night when I opened my eyes. I could hear the footsteps and voices of people walking along the road. Most of them were civilians, but some were soldiers. I stayed in the dream world, but I didn't leave until it was too late. However, I was in trouble in the bush because I wasn't hiding at all. People saw me, but believed I was dead. I waited for them. I stood up when they came to the crossroads, and followed the path to Nyamata. At least, I recognized the cables that ran near Kurarete (Kigali to Nyamata). I followed them until I reached Nyirarukobwa. Although I felt dizzy from hunger, I continued to push my body until the end. I marched on until I reached the forest. On the path, I saw a woman and a man. These were likely Hutus. They spoke and seemed unaffected by the Tutsi killings in the vicinity. I turned around. I continued looking for the electrical cables that would allow me to return home. I was able to pass behind some bushes. I finally reached the Kayumba Eucalyptus Forest. I was extremely cautious and suspicious of any movement that I could hear or see. I saw a group as I climbed the hill from the forest. I slowed down, and I went behind a small bush. I continued to observe them and realized that some of them were severely injured.

They are Tutsis! That was what I thought.

They approached me. They were so happy to see me, as I was the only one in the middle of nowhere. It was a surprise to see the young man, who had been there the night before and ran after me like an antelope hunting a hyena.

"How did that soldier escape you yesterday?" I was happy to meet someone I knew, and I asked him. I didn't recognize the other.

"I ran and, after a few metres, I moved off the road and hugged an enormous tree. I was right next to the soldier!" The young man I was talking to, whose name I forgot, because at that time memorizing names didn't mean anything. We had made it clear that we were ready to die and not live.

Some Tutsis from the area had survived the massacre at Nyamata Church. Others had blood on their bodies like me. Others sustained serious injuries. All were very tired and quiet. As I wanted to return home, I told my friend that I was going to Nyirarukobwa but would be back. I wasn't looking for electrical cables anymore because I had reached Nyamata forest, where we had fled to Nyamata the day before.

My friend was with another group young boys and I said, "See you later.".

I chose the Nyirarukobwa path. I was walking along the path to Nyirarukobwa when I noticed a terrible stench. I didn't know what it was, but I kept going. Two old men lay down when I arrived at the spot where Maliya, my dad and other Tutsis fled to Kayumba forest. I tried to approach them but they grew more foul-smelling the closer I got. They were probably dead while we fled to Nyamata, I discovered. Their bodies were decaying, and the stench of death was everywhere. It was horrible.

I continued toward Nyirarukobwa. I passed by that bush where Kabanda, Callixte and my father had hidden their belongings, including beds, clothes and other things. I saw that they were dislodged, possibly by plundering Hutus; some of the things like the mattress and bed had been taken. I headed to Nyirarukobwa. From Kayumba Hill I could see Nyirarukobwa, our old school. I saw a few people in the school compound. When I got closer, I heard voices behind the school. Passing through the small forest, I came near the home of an old man who was living in the swamp. His name was Ruterana, and he was the guardian of our school.

I saw a dead body on the ground so I changed direction. I felt I was in danger. I feared I would be caught by the men talking at the school; people so carefree sounding could not be Tutsis. I continued on my way home, passing by Nyamihana's water pump, the place where we used to fetch water. There were no people around. Finally, I reached home. I opened the door and went inside. Our house did not seem like it had been attacked. We had rabbits, and before my dad left, he had put them in the sitting room. When they saw me, they came up to me: they were probably very hungry. I was also hungry. I

went into our kitchen garden and brought a lot of vegetables for the four rabbits. They ate as children at a party. It was sad to look at them; I was thinking that I could not stay long since the house was not safe. Tutsis were being hunted everywhere: houses, bushes, forests, swamps, hills, anywhere they could flee to.

I left home with much sadness, trying to impress on my mind the last image of a place where I had smiled and seen my whole family smile. I went to Callixte's house. Arriving at *ku irembo* (their gate), I understood why, the other day, I had waited for my father until late at night. I found a lot of things in the compound, including my father's Quran. Hutus had attacked their house and taken almost everything. Their door was wide open, with total silence within. I continued to Kabanda's house. Their house was a little bit bigger and closed. I did not enter as I was very scared. I continued to Simeon's house, a Tutsi who was Kabanda's neighbour. No one was there. I really don't remember why I continued to inspect those houses, perhaps I was simply a lonely boy in a deserted neighbourhood. I passed through a banana plantation before I reached another house, Kamali's, who was living next to Foramina's family. All of these people were Tutsis. I saw a movement at the back of the house. My heart started pounding because I had not really seen what that flash of motion was. I went into the sorghum around the house, looking through the *imiyenzi* fence. I saw two old men with machetes. My heart was beating faster and faster. I could not run to escape them, so I stayed hidden. They entered the compound from the backyard of the house and took the *ingunguru* (a metal barrel) and then went back. I thanked God for having saved me again.

Kamali had an orange tree, and all the children in the village used to go there and take oranges in the season. I went towards the tree, but the oranges were not yet ripe. I was still very hungry. Using a baton, I pulled down a lot of green oranges and started eating them without removing their peels. As Kinyarwanda used to say, "*Haryoha Inzara*".

I sat down and ate. The tree was not far from the main road from Kigali to Nyamata. After half an hour, I saw five men walking on the road from the direction of Kurarete. As they reached Kabanda's land, I closely observed them. In their hands I saw machetes and hoes used for digging. They were moving very quickly. I started hearing voices and screams from very far away, from the direction of Ntarama.

"Oh my God, I am in danger!" I murmured to myself.

I laid in the grass under the orange tree but kept my eye on those Hutus who were passing on the road. When they were far enough from my hiding place, I quickly left the area. I never returned to those houses again but decided to go towards Kayumba. Running without shoes over stones and on grass, I went to Nyamihana's water pump to drink water. Soon after I was lost in the bushes. I could only hear birds.

As I reached the bush where our family had hidden our property, I took Maliya's *Kitenge*, the catechism book, and a rosary. I did not mind that I had been raised a Muslim. I knew that I could die anytime and praying was my only comfort, as I knew that if I died at least I would be going to heaven. I would speak to God in any language he would listen to! Before reaching the forest, I met Kabyina Bahishije, a young man who was my classmate.

"Hello, Kabyina, where are you going?" I asked him, very happy to meet someone I knew.

He was not sure where to go, nor was I. We separated. He continued toward Nyirarukobwa, and I went back. I wanted to join those Tutsi refugees I had left in the forest. I wanted to be with that young man who had struggled like me during the Nyamata massacre; he was the only person I had left from there. I found them still there, inside the forest. My friend had started to talk with two other young boys whose parents were living in a place called Rwakibilizi. They wanted to go with him to their home to get a coat and some bed covers. The young man had already been convinced to go with them and wanted me to go along. But I was afraid because we could be killed on the way. As they insisted, we finally agreed to go there in the evening, as it was a little bit safer to travel then. They had convinced me that their father was still at home and that he would give us food and bed covers. I could not refuse. It was the fourth day without any food, and it was the rainy season, so it got very cold during the night.

Eventually, the evening came. As the road was not very safe, our preferred way to travel was to pass through the bushes. We finally reached Nyamata, ending up behind APEBU. APEBU was a private school built by Tutsis in Nyamata to enable their children to attend secondary school. We continued on our way to Rwakibilizi, passing through a forest that was below ADPR hospital. As it was very dark, we did not continue to those two boys' home. The elder was John. He was the oldest of all of us. He said we should go into the cassava trees below the street leading to their home. Those cassava trees were very close, to find a place to sleep in the middle of them was difficult, besides, we were very hungry. John, his brother, and my friend got some cassava roots. We ate them in the dark and then slept. As I was the only one with a *Kitenge*, I slept in the middle and we all covered ourselves with it. We had no other choice but to sleep and let mosquitoes bite us. The next morning, we were awakened by the bicycle bells of young Hutus going to Rwakibilizi to fetch water. We ate a few more cassava roots and continued to the house. We could not use the road, only pass through the sorghum. Their house had been burnt down along with everything inside it. Their relatives, who had mental health issues, had been killed in the backyard. I could see the sorrow in John and his brother's eyes.

10 LIFE IN RWAKIBILIZI

In this ruined home in Rwakibilizi, we were not safe. Crying didn't feel right, everyone among us knew that he could be next. Trying to save our lives was the only right thing to do. We passed in front of their house, crossed the street and went through John's parents' land. They had planted avocadoes, sorghum and sweet potatoes. We found some avocados that had fallen down. It was

God sending free food to us disparate young boys. We grabbed them and started eating.

They were delicious or, as Rwandans say, "hungry delicious". After eating, we walked between John's parents' land and some small bushes close to their garden. We settled ourselves inside a bush. During the genocide, bushes, and sorghum were safer than houses. We started our life of homelessness there, in cold and heavy rain. These were the lesser evils, the weather wasn't menacing our lives, however, it gave me a bad cough that could betray our presence. Anytime Interahamwe might find us and slaughter us like hunted animals. Those three boys wanted me to hide in a separate bush as I could blow their cover, but I asked to remain with them. Finally they let me, perhaps because I had the *Kitenge*.

Our nights were days and our days were nights; we were sleeping during the day and went out during the night to dig up sweet potatoes. We would wake up after some time to eat again. When it rained, we would stand or sit closer to each other to reduce the cold. How did we reach this point? How could we suffer just because we were born Tutsi? None of us knew how to answer these questions. Praying was my occupation. Repenting my sins and asking God's pardon were my favourite prayers. The items I had brought with me were all I owned. In our existence, where the life expectancy was one day if not one minute, everything I could use to talk to God was valuable to me. In my heart, I knew I was a true and convinced Muslim, but in the absence of the Quran, I didn't mind praying in a Catholic way, using a rosary and a Christian book. It was not an issue of which belief was true to God. I came to understand in those dark moments that religion belongs to me and not me to religion. But why talk to God? My father along with many other Tutsis had been butchered in the same Catholic church that had seen them baptized along with those who had butchered them. I spent my days reading my catechism book, reciting the rosary and promising God that if he saved me from the death I saw, I would forever be grateful to him.

Life was not easy at all. The rain became very intense. One day, we shifted and went back to John's parents' house. John's parents had left behind some cooked yellow maize flour (*pate jaune*), which had been thrown on the floor during the raid on the house. Part of the food had been damaged by the rain and some had been contaminated by small insects called *inshishi*. We removed the insects and ate. I could not imagine how that food would have tasted if we had not been so hungry. It shows how inhuman one can become, eating dust to save one's life. After all, in the eyes of the killers we were less than humans and deserved only to be cut into pieces.

My cough had worsened because of the rain and the nights spent in the bushes. We had found a strategy to hide from the Hutu women who came during the daylight to pick cassava leaves (*isombe*) and sweet potatoes from John's parents' land. I would cover my whole head with *igitenge* with the help of the boys who were tightening it around my mouth to ensure I didn't make a noise. What stress I was causing those boys, who were almost brothers to me. They did this the whole time I spent at Rwakibilizi. Only God knows how I can pay them back. Even if it was just a small act of kindness, I will forever be thankful to them because coughing could have cost me my life as well as theirs.

One day in the bush, a wounded man appeared. He was hidden not far from us. "*Hano hari umuntu ukorora cyane bazabafata babicire hano*" (Here there is someone who is coughing, they will find you and kill you), he said.

I was terrified that my friends would push me away to hide by myself in another bush.

But John said, "From now on, every time you are going to cough, I will help you cover your mouth."

"Thank you!" I responded without hesitation.

We gave sweet potatoes to the man. After eating, he hid in a bush above where we were living. His leg had been seriously injured; he had made a makeshift crutch out of a piece of wood. It was a terrible life: we spent a whole week eating uncooked sweet potatoes and drinking rainwater. Life was more than miserable with the constant threat of death. I could see no way out, trapped in that jungle of devils where human beings were forced to become animals; where living in bushes was preferable to living in houses because having a home was not our privilege. We deserved to die, that is what

Habyarimana and his men made those who were hunting us day after day believe. After several days in those bushes, one morning we heard the voices of men who had come with dogs. They found the man and beat him.

"Uziko hano harimo abantu?" (There are people hiding here?) one of them asked while they were beating him. As they were speaking, the dog barked. We came out of our bush and started crawling away to escape them. Luckily enough, those Interahamwe did not follow us, they were busy killing the man.

I am not sure if he survived or not. We were followed by their dogs, while they remained. Whether he died or miraculously survived, my God please put his name among those whom you will take to heaven. We ran back towards John's parents' house. One man saw us, but fortunately he did not follow us. We entered a field of sorghum. We hid there, in a hole dug for erosion water control. I had left in the bush my three precious things, my catechism book, my rosary and my *kitenge*. Nevertheless, praying remained on my to-do list as it was my only refuge during that time of darkness, at the mercy of animals disguised as humans. Because of hunger, most of our time was spent sleeping in the afternoon. We slept in our new hiding place, under the trees inside the field of sorghum. I slept in the middle. Luckily enough, it was not raining in this new place. We could not find anything to eat, though. What we had experienced in the morning was not yet over in my mind and I struggled to fall asleep.

That afternoon, I heard a loud sound from the sorghum trees as if someone was walking through them. When I looked through the plants, I saw a man with a dark face and red eyes coming toward us. Interahamwe! We were being attacked again. "Wake up!" I told my friends. They were in a deep sleep. I moved to the right, trying to get out of those trees. My friends took the opposite direction. I saw a group of young Interahamwe Hutu militiamen with machetes.

They started to chant, "Ahoo ahoo!" (Stay there, stay there!) I had nowhere to go, but after some seconds of reflecting, I ran back to the erosion control hole. I debated whether it was worth trying to stay alive or if I should give up. When I got there, I was alone. My friends were gone, that Hutu man had run after them screaming. When that group of young Interahamwe heard their comrades running after my friends, they followed them. I remained alone in that field of sorghum. I still don't understand how that was possible. I saw God's hand intervening in my life!

Left on the ridge alone, I was discouraged. I was fed up with this life of hiding. I decided to stop and go back to Kayumba. I had decided that being killed wouldn't terrify me anymore. I was alone, I had lost the only friends I had. We had suffered together for such a long time, in heavy rain, sun and cold. I had nothing left, so I left the sorghum plantation and started walking on the road from Rwakibirizi. On my way, I meet young Hutus on bicycles. They were going to fetch water. The first few I met did nothing, they were in a rush, but I had decided to die anyway. I knew that at any time they could stop and kill me. Before I became a cloud of dust, I would go in the direction of Kayumba.

"Ubwo nturi Umututsi. ubwo nturi Inkotanyi sha?" (Aren't you Tutsi *Inkotanyi*?) asked a young Hutu boy, who was on a bicycle with his friends.

"Hoya sindiyo" (No, I am not), I replied, not sure if they were going to accept that as an answer.

They continued on their way. After few metres, I met another group of youths on bicycles.

"Nturi Umututsi sha?" (Aren't you Tutsi?) "No,"

I said to them.

"Why that blood on your clothes?"

"I don't know," I replied.

I reached a village with a few houses behind the Sous prefecture of Kanazi office. There were not so many people, just some Hutu women with their children. When they saw me, they screamed loudly, *"Muze murebe agakotanyi, muze murebe agakotanyi"* (Come and see that small *Inkotanyi!*)

I never heard more tormenting words than those. The women and small children kept calling their neighbours.

"Muze murebe agakotanyi booboo..." (Come and see this small *Inkotanyi* booboo...)

I felt cold and terrified. I decided not to run away as that would encourage them to run after me and kill me on the street. Probably, they were calling their husbands or young Interahamwe to do the job. I continued on through that dehumanizing crowd until I had left the neighbourhood. When I was about to reach Nyamata central town, I saw a giant man who was fetching water from a public water pump.

"Come here, you, young man!" he said me.

"No, I can't," I replied.

I suspected that he wanted to kill me, and I decided to disobey him. He could have run after me, but he didn't. Only God knows why. I was at their mercy. I realized that even children, who are born innocent, and women, who give life, had no pity after they had dehumanized me on the street.

11 RETURNING TO KAYUMBA HILL

On that day, that very sunny day, with the sunset kissing the trees and bushes on the calm hills, far from the screams of innocent souls slaughtered like animals, I returned to Kayumba Hill. I had already left that hill twice, always ending up with shattered hopes. My life was no longer mine. I wanted to end my journey. I was fed up with being hunted like antelopes in a field, especially after leaving that village near Nyamata, where women and children had humiliated me so.

I was scared but I found out that ending my life and my journey wasn't an easy wish. I realized that I was reaching the extreme point of my painful life: hunger had left my body, which was no longer resisting the harsh wind. I was overwhelmed, thinking about the ones I had lost and kept losing in front of my eyes. I no longer felt human, I kept thinking about dead bodies. I was living with the thought of them and always meeting new corpses while hiding; their smell was my reminder that tomorrow it could be me in their place. It wasn't easy.

On my way to Kayumba, I met a couple, a woman and a man talking about Nyamata business centre without worries. They were Hutus. How lucky they were, not being hunted like me. I hoped they would not use their time to kill, that they might not have seen me. I continued on my way to Kayumba in a silent mood. My mind was full of questions and painful memories of thousands of souls lost before my eyes. A few metres from that couple, I found the dead body of a man. His body was decomposing. The sight was as horrible as the smell. Covering my nose with my t-shirt was the only solution as I had to pass that dead man, killed like many other Tutsis, whose corpses were left everywhere, in the hills, swamps, forests and bushes. Everywhere smelled like death. For me it was everywhere, as I was traveling and sleeping in the same T-shirt and shorts soaked in the blood of Nyamata Church.

After crossing the road to Nyamata near AJEPO, I saw a group of four young cowboys, sitting on the grass at sunset looking after their cows. They turned their eyes towards me. Although they did not attack me, I hurried up to Kayumba because I thought they would run after me. I started running, climbing hills, hiding behind bush after bush, coming up only to be sure of where I was going. I was uncertain whether I could reach the first hill of Kayumba before getting killed on the way. I had had enough of tragedies, and I was living every day like it was my last. Finally, I reached Kayumba.

Returning from Rwakibilizi was another miracle in that dark April of 1994. In Rwanda, it was another form of torture. But this time was particularly cruel because women, together with children, had decided to attack a child like theirs, like them. How accurate was my friend Sarah Brown when she wrote her PhD thesis; the dissertation was about Rwandan women who could be mothers, wives, sisters, daughters and, at the same time, *genocidaires*, a common term used to define the perpetrators of Rwanda genocide.

I passed near the houses of Hutus who could have killed me, but didn't. The same happened with the young Hutus I met on my way to Kayumba. During these hopeless days, God was looking out for me.

Reaching Kayumba, the situation had changed. I knew no one there. I spotted some survivors who were still struggling with life in the jungle; some of them had children, others were injured and had machete wounds on their bodies. Eating was a nightmare. Everyone was cooking for their children; some people who knew each other were cooking in groups. It was a daily struggle. Every day was somebody's last day; someone who might have made a very cold evening a warm one could be just another sad story the next evening. Every day we were hunted by Interahamwe.

My first night after I returned to Kayumba, I joined a group of Tutsis in the middle of Kayumba forest. I started telling some of them what had happened during the time I had spent in Rwakibilizi. Luckily enough, when the time came, we ate in a group. That evening felt like a miracle to me, as it had been a long time since I had eaten cooked food. People were telling story after story as a way of keeping their minds busy, because not very far from where we were sitting in the forest, bodies of killed Tutsis were scattered everywhere. Night fell, and we slept on the grass near the place where we had cooked the food. The next morning, people cooked again while we were preparing to go hiding. When the food was almost ready, we heard rifle shots. "*Interahamwe ziraje!*" (Interahamwe are coming!) somebody said.

We all ran towards Nyirarukobwa, leaving the food. We hid in the sorghum fields. People were going everywhere: I was with two women and the three children of one of them. We stayed there until we heard that things had calmed down. We waited for the evening to go back to the forest.

When we got back, everything was destroyed. The food was thrown on the ground, and the pot used to cook was crushed. I stayed with that woman; she became a sort of stepmother to me since I could easily ask her for food. In the evening, she asked me to go fetch some water for cooking. I accepted straight away. I went with other, older people and children. We brought water from the swamp, but my *igicuma* (Natural gourd for water), which I was using to ferry water, had holes in it.

I came back with wet clothes and very little water. I was hungry but, knowing no one, I started to overthink things, hating what my life had become. In the evening, we changed place. Interahamwe had killed people and destroyed everything from the previous day, and it had rained. We were still inside the forest. Our night was during daybreak because at night it was safer to travel, although we had nowhere to go.

That night was very short as people were exchanging stories about what everyone had gone through during the day. The next morning, I joined the woman again because she had a very young baby and a child and needed help. We left the forest to hide inside some cassava trees, but when there she asked us to leave that place and go into the sorghum field, which was nearby. Lice in my clothes (*Inda*) were biting me, and I could no longer resist the pain when we reached the sorghum. I removed my clothes and started to kill the insects. I was hungry and terrified that Interahamwe would find us and kill us. Everyone hid alone to avoid them. They could find us as a group, but I didn't care. During the day, two men passed near our hiding place. They were about to enter the sorghum field when one of them said: "I don't think you will find them here."

"Oh my God, save me, and I will pray to you forever" was my silent prayer before going to sleep every night.

We moved out of the field at noon and went to the hill near the forest. I was hungry. I don't know how I fell asleep, but while I was sleeping, I started to see the sky moving and had a strange dream. It soon turned out to be real: Interahamwe were attacking. Previously, men had stayed behind to form a line of resistance while women and children had run. This time I thought I might stay with the men. After a while we heard whistles and knew the Interahamwe had come. We ran, as women and children had had time to get away already. Men with machetes pursued me as I desperately ran through the forest full of dead bodies, and they were catching up as I was weak from hunger. I blamed myself for not running earlier, with the women and children. As I burst out of the forest, another miracle happened. The Tutsi men had formed a line brandishing sharpened wooden sticks and other traditional weapons and were ready to fight. I summoned whatever energy I had left and made it through, a machete almost catching me. When the Interahamwe saw the Tutsis running towards them, they turned around and fled.

"You were going to be killed!" they exclaimed.

I thanked God yet again.

Every day at Kayumba Hill was similar to the previous one. Interahamwe came every day, running after us, capturing small groups of Tutsis and killing them, leaving their bodies in the forest without burying them. Some memories of Kayumba stayed in my mind and have never left.

I remember a woman who had a deaf and dumb brother. She did everything for her brother, always cooking food, and running with him whenever they needed to hide. In the evening, she would return with her brother and cook for him, and they would sleep late. They talked to each other using signs; she loved her brother a lot. I was delighted to see the way she was taking care of him. One evening she did not come back, and Dumb (as we used to call him) spent the evening asking everyone where his sister was. None of us had the answer until we saw her body the next day. That marked me: although I had lost every hope for myself, I often thought about the dumb boy and the way his sister loved him and treated him! A few days later, he followed his sister in death. It remained something that had touched my heart. We talked about them, we were all sad, thinking that our survival was also not guaranteed. They were killed at a time when the attacks had subsided, although we did not know why.

Life in Kayumba was a nightmare for me as a child with no relatives. I was an orphan in the jungle. There were people who took pity on me and I owe them some recognition in this account; they were selfless back in those dark days of our lives. Some died in the forest, others survived. Kayumba became our home.

12 INKOTANYI ZAJE!

The attacks gradually stopped, thus we left the forest and went to live in a house near the forest. In the distance, we could see masses of people leaving. They were soldiers who were fleeing to Burundi. We did not know what was taking place nor why the attacks had decreased. Some slept in the house while others, like me, were spending the night in the cows' outhouse. One day, when we were coming from the sorghum fields, I saw people removing the body of a young boy who had died. Some were saying that he had had a lot of food the day before, having spent many days without eating. May God give him peace together with ours. As everyone thought that we would die soon as well, none of us cried for that boy. We spent a whole day without an attack. In the evening, we returned to where we had spent the previous night. The men had brought cassava and *amateke*. While we were about to start cooking, two boys came from the banana trees saying, "*Inkotanyi* are here to save us!"

"Are you sure or is it a strategy by Interahamwe to catch us and kill us all?"

Some old men asked the boys to go and see if they were really *Inkotanyi*. I decided to remain, peeling vegetables. Two boys came back to tell us that *Inkotanyi* were in Kayumba forest and that they were rescuing people. We ran without looking back. As I was hungry, I took two cassavas to eat along the way. In the forest, we found a line of *Inkotanyi*: they were checking us before helping people and making them join other small groups of survivors. RPA[1] soldiers were confiscating the traditional weapons Tutsis had used to resist the attacks.

In what looked like an evening of hope, the darkness in Kayumba forest was lit up by RPF soldiers' torch lights. They were searching for survivors and the path to Nyamata. After the survivors had been gathered in the forest, we headed to Nyamata. Those who were not wounded or seriously wounded marched on their own. On our way, we found other small groups of rescued survivors. I was happy that we were rescued but also still in deep shock. On our way we stopped in a street within the ADPR fence, a site which was to become a hospital. Escorted by RPA soldiers, we continued to Nyamata town. There they took us to the Mingeti orphanage. The orphans were sharing rooms to make space for the survivors.

We were not far from the church. The victims had been buried in mass graves, with a bulldozer covering their bodies with soil. The grave formed a small hill behind the church.

RPA soldiers were distributing clothes. I got two shorts and two t-shirts. I removed my old clothes and threw them by the gate, after one month and thirteen days without washing or changing them. They were full of lice and blood. Some soldiers had pitched tents outside the orphanage to protect us. Inside, people were happy, some even crying tears of joy. Others were eating biscuits given to them by the soldiers. At midnight, soldiers brought barrels of cooked rice. We ate all the food brought by them, until we had had enough and were no longer hungry; it was the first time since the genocide began.

Our first night without fearing to be killed the next day was very fascinating. Women, men, and children were all in the same hall. None of us could believe it after living life like hunted animals. The next day, I was enrolled in the orphanage and spent two days there. On the third day, in the evening after the prayers (the orphanage belonged to the Catholic Church), when we were going to eat, someone came up to my table and told me, "*Hari umuntu ugushaka hanze!*" (Someone wants you outside!)

I had convinced myself that I was alone in this world. Learning that someone had asked for me was a shock. I was so surprised. I thought everyone had died! When I reached the door I found Uwamaliya Renatha. She hugged me. She was equally happy to see someone from her family who had survived! I was speechless and reluctant to leave the orphanage, but she insisted that I go with her. She had survived along with her husband Habarugira and her lastborn son Lambert. They were living in *mukibikira* (convent) as place was called with a lot of other families, men were spending the night in a communal room while children and women had their own room. I saw a lot of people I recognized. The first night there, everyone was talking about who had survived. "At Bernard's house, Kaunda has survived…" I was very tired and soon fell asleep.

The next day some of the assembled families decided to occupy empty houses, mostly belonging to the government. Rulangirwanda's family occupied Kanzenze Court House, while we moved to a house near Kanzenze

Tribunal Court and Nyamata Hospital. We were three families in one house. Stories of the genocide were present in every discussion. Habarugira was known in the whole of Bugesera as he had led the resistance at Ntarama swamp, and been the only one in possession of a gun after having confiscated the weapon from an attacking policeman. Habarugira was and will remain a hero for those who survived in Bugesera.

13 A LIFE OF FLASHBACKS

After the genocide, Habyarimana's photo was still present in many houses, mostly governmental buildings. I remember that the next morning someone climbed a wooden stepladder (*urwego*) and took down a photo. Children would jump on them, tearing them into pieces and throwing them in the dustbin. It was the start of a new life, although still a life of uncertainty. I could not imagine what the future would look like. This life was not easy; we were three families in one house, squeezed together.

Searching for firewood and going to Nyamabuye, Rwangara, Kayumba and Rwakibirizi to find food in the fields (*Imirima*), accompanied by Garukurore and my cousin Claude Shimwa, were my daily tasks. We always went in big groups, as we were still wary of Interahamwe and traumatised by what we had gone through. One day, Claude saw a military car and went with the soldiers. He didn't come back until two years later.

In this strange life, where everything was broken, where women, men and children were sleeping in the same room, we were trying to forge a new life as survivors. Thousands of Tutsis who had fled to Burundi since 1959 were coming back. These refugees were coming in big vehicles while the military were also bringing other rescued people to Nyamata as it was considered a safe place. Survivors came in military cars from Kigali to meet surviving relatives. All in all, many were coming to Nyamata! Wounded and sick people were being treated in the convent near the church.

One day as I was taking food for Ndashimye Garukurore's son, who was in the hospital, I passed the road where we had run from the commune to the church. For a brief moment, I was living in my past, while others were seeing only an empty street!

Arriving at the hospital, one could see how the genocide had devastated Rwanda. The room where Ndashimye was being treated was also occupied by wounded people from the genocide as well as used as a maternity ward! Taboos and norms no longer existed. While I was there, a pregnant woman was giving a birth and I remember men and women using *Kitenges* to form a delivery room! That woman's cries reminded me of everything I had seen in the church. I left the place and went back home.

Many journalists were coming to Nyamata. One day one came to talk to a woman who was living with us, she had also survived the Nyamata Church massacre. The interview took place in the church. While she was talking I interrupted them every few minutes, as I really wanted to tell them my story.

I tried to avoid anything that could remind me of my parents or my brother and sister because I thought that everyone was dead. When people from Kigali began to arrive in Bugesera, they told Uwamaliya and Habarugira that my mum was still alive. When they told me this, I thought about it and decided that I knew she was dead; they were lying. I could not see how she could have survived. One day, I was playing with other children far from home when, suddenly, one of my peers told me, "Please get back home, they want you." I ignored him as our game was very exciting, and it was helping me not to think about what I had lived through during the genocide. Then a second boy said, "Please go back home, your mum wants to see you!"

"My mum!" I ran home and entered the house. I still remember that when I saw her, I was not able to say anything. Nor was she, for she was crying. We hugged. Inside I was overjoyed but torn between two extremes, total sadness and complete happiness. It made me speechless. She had come to pick me up to go to Kigali. There was no regular transport, so it was a matter of waiting for soldiers going in that direction.

The next day my mum and I waited until the afternoon to get a military car. Luckily, we found a Daihatsu. I was very excited, I wanted to sit like soldiers sit in their cars. On our way to Kigali, the car had technical problems. We went back to Nyamata. We heard that there was a catholic brother who had come to Bugesera to see his mother and sister who had survived. They were going to Kigali, so we joined them. Life after genocide was governed by random events.

In Kigali we spent a night at the Jesuit Monastery of Remera. The next day, we left for my mum's house in Samuduha. She had survived along with my sister; it was another miracle. She had been hidden by a Hutu family, never leaving the house. Her hiding places were under a bed and under a big basket in the garden. I left Bugesera never thinking I would go back there ever again. What I had seen, heard and lost their amounted to almost my whole life. Luckily, I was starting another chapter of my new life. A life against all odds. If it had not been for the heroism of my mum, I could have become something else, lost my way, but I was so lucky that my life went back to normal.

I went back to school one year after the genocide. School was hard. I realized that I was not ready and was totally devastated. Trying to adapt to a normal life was difficult. After three months of study, I passed my remaining term in the school year that had so cruelly been cut short. I struggled to concentrate. I kept failing the following year, but my mother never gave up on me and kept pushing.

My mother decide that we were to move back to Bugesera in 1996. Me and my sister went to Cyugaro Primary School. Not only was this school very far away but it was also near Ntarama Genocide Memorial. I was scared of failing and wanted to repeat an earlier year. I kept thinking of my father urging me to be strong and felt like I was betraying him. I asked my mum to go back in P2 instead of primary 5 and my sister in P1 instead of P3, my mum eventually agreed that I could restart Year 3, and my sister also repeated a year. Such are the consequences of what we had gone through.

My school in Nyirarukobwa had been totally destroyed during the genocide, and the circa 95 families living nearby had been wiped out. This became the source of my determination to pass in class! I wanted to tell my story and write a history of hope, keeping the memory of those we lost alive forever. My first year at Cyugaro I passed with 94%. I never considered the deep poverty we were living in, sometimes spending a day without eating, and how far we had to run to get to school.

In 1998 my mum took us back to Kigali where I finished primary school. I studied Human Science at secondary school and when I passed the National Exam as second of our class it became my first step out of that dark tunnel I was in. I enrolled at university at the Kigali Institute of Education, where I studied economics and education.

Though we were poor, I was determined to succeed, to prove that there is light at the end of the tunnel. I wanted to live a life that reflects God's greatness, a life of working hard. I can't thank God enough for having rescued me from those bloody and dark times. This book is for those silenced souls buried in churches, mass graves, former communes' offices and houses, halls and hospitals. I hope that by sharing this story we can learn to prevent similar atrocities from happening in the future.

14 ENDING WITH HOPE

How do you end a story like the one of surviving a genocide? Because a genocide never ends, may it be the one in Germany, where they used gas chambers, or the one in Rwanda, where they used machetes, guns and wooden clubs. All of those killing instruments might have been burnt and buried in genocide memorials but is that enough to close stories like these? I guess the response may vary.

While writing this excerpt of my life, I chose to end it with hope, a hope which is not an ephemeral one because this book is an existing sign that life won over evil, because I, along with others, survived to tell our story.

It is the hope I expressed during all those years before this book came out. Poverty at its extreme level had occupied our home. During those days I went to school with less interest, I missed class after class. Two years after the genocide, my mother kept telling me that I shouldn't be among the losers. I also remembered the words of my father, "Uzabe Umugabo" (Be strong). That is the same message I want to leave you with.

When I started to write this book, I was more than passionate to write about the genocide, for me, as a survivor, it was like therapy. The same hope underwrote my passion to work, empowering me, and spurring me on to engage with young people. I couldn't end this story with the machete seasons that ruined my childhood and killed my people. I hate numbers because their deaths were not just numbers. I preferred to end this book with hope. I want to defeat that ideology which was to exterminate my people until their names remained only in books of history as none of them was supposed to escape and tell his own story.

* * *

While writing this story, I learnt that my child self-died at ten years old, during the genocide. This account not only became my therapy but also my chance to meet with you, reader. I believe that the more pages of this book you read, the more you discussed with me and helping me putting up with my past, because the more I was writing, the more I was sharing and releasing the past from my mind. Isn't that hope?

The answer may vary, again, but through sharing this story, I found the motivation behind my passion of always accepting challenges as an opportunity to find new solutions because I realized that after surviving a genocide the best choice is to live and not to merely survive.

During my university studies, I was a member of AERG,[1] a student association for survivors, which I led two years as second vice coordinator until 2011.

The same message of hope is at the centre of Humura Nturi Wenyine, which means "don't worry, you are not alone", an initiative using volunteers trained in trauma healing to support people with trauma and going through emotional crises. I conceived this programme with some colleagues after attending the commemoration of the genocide in Amahoro Stadium in Kigali, where a young woman, who was sitting near me, got affected by an emotional crisis. Everyone wanted to run away, before a young man decided to help her in that very difficult situation, as she was screaming that Interahamwe were going to kill her.

The episode made me reflect on my life in Nyamata and those of other survivors, who had nowhere to escape that hunting traumatic past. Still a student at the time, I was wondering, how do you survive killers who hunt you in your memories? I was amazed by how the members of our National Committee agreed to this idea.

I needed to tell, to write and to work on this very sad past and let everyone know about it. Is surviving a genocide the most traumatic event possible?

Maybe not, but when I saw Humura Nturi Wenyine and other initiatives, such as free phone lines that act as safe spaces to share psychological wounds and various forms of legal support, I was more than happy. And grateful as well to those who served along with me when I was still a student at university. This aftermath was owed to my ten-year-old self that I lost.

I am aware that it is an attempt to reclaim that glorious age that I lost in that dark church in Nyamata. Again, this book remains a beacon of hope that our lives will live eternally, from our hearts, from generations to generations, because hope is the only thing left to those who survive and choose to live life beyond fear, pain and loss.